Trucks

Chris Oxlade

Heinemann
LIBRARY

www.heinemann.co.uk
Visit our website to find out more information about Heinemann Library books.

To order:

 Phone 44 (0) 1865 888066

 Send a fax to 44 (0) 1865 314091

Visit the Heinemann Bookshop at www.heinemann.co.uk to browse our catalogue and order online.

First published in Great Britain by Heinemann Library, Halley Court, Jordan Hill, Oxford OX2 8EJ a division of Reed Educational and Professional Publishing Ltd.
Heinemann is a registered trademark of Reed Educational & Professional Publishing Ltd.

OXFORD MELBOURNE AUCKLAND
JOHANNESBURG BLANTYRE GABORONE
IBADAN PORTSMOUTH (NH) USA CHICAGO

Designed by Paul Davies and Associates
Originated by Ambassador Litho Ltd
Printed in Hong Kong/China

05 04 03 02 01
10 9 8 7 6 5 4 3 2 1

ISBN 0431 10855 2

British Library Cataloguing in Publication Data

Oxlade, Chris
 Trucks. – (Transport around the world)
 1.Trucks – Juvenile literature
 2.Transportation, Automotive – Juvenile literature
 I.Title
 629.2'24

Acknowledgements
The Publishers would like to thank the following for permission to reproduce photographs:
R D Battersby pp4, 15, 26; Trevor Clifford p10; Corbis p22; David Hoffman p23; Eye Ubiquitous pp9, 11, 13, 14, 16, 29; Pictures p27; Quadrant pp7, 12, 17, 18, 19, 24, 28; Science & Society Picture Library p8; Swift: Peter Sawell & Partners/Freight Transport Association p6; Travel Ink: Tony Page p5; Tony Stone Images pp20, 25; John Walmsley p21

Cover photograph reproduced with permission of Tony Stone Images

Every effort has been made to contact copyright holders of any material reproduced in this book. Any omissions will be rectified in subsequent printings if notice is given to the Publisher.

Contents

Any words appearing in the text in bold, **like this**, are explained in the glossary.

What is a truck?

A truck is a large vehicle that moves along on wheels. Trucks carry goods called **cargo**. At the front of the truck is a **cab** where the driver sits. At the back is a big space for the cargo.

4

Cargo is being loaded on to this truck. The truck will carry the heavy cargo safely to where it is needed. Then the cargo will be unloaded again.

How trucks work

A truck has an **engine** that makes its wheels turn to move it along. The engine needs to be powerful to move the heavy **cargo**. It needs **fuel** to make it work.

Trucks have wheels that go round. Each wheel has a **rubber tyre** around it. Small trucks have four wheels. Some big trucks have twelve wheels or even more.

Old trucks

This truck is almost 100 years old. It was one of the first trucks with an **engine**. The engine is a **steam** engine, like the ones used in steam trains. Before engines, horses and wagons transported **cargo**.

This small truck was made in America in the 1930s. It is called a pick-up truck. It has a **petrol** engine instead of a steam engine. Today many people drive modern pick-up trucks.

Where are trucks used?

Big trucks like this one carry **cargo** along main roads between towns and cities. The smooth, hard road surface allows the trucks to travel quickly.

Some trucks go through areas where there are no roads, or just dirt tracks. The ground can get very muddy. The drivers must know how to drive safely over rough ground.

Flatbed trucks

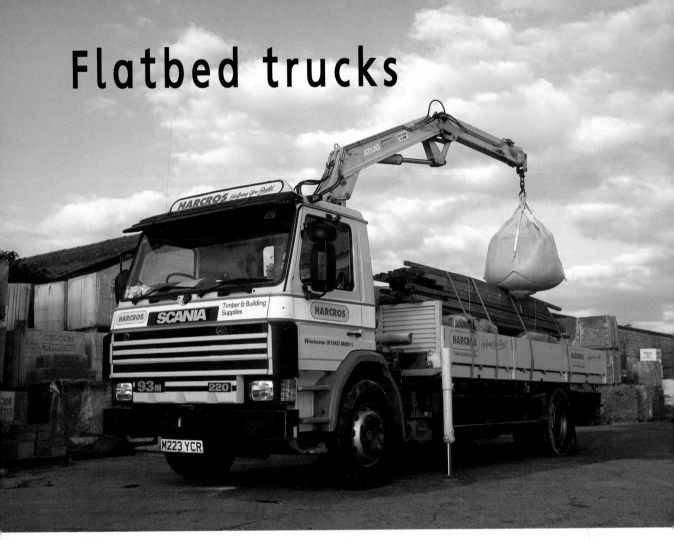

A truck with a flat **cargo** space is called a flatbed truck. It can carry almost any sort of cargo. The cargo is tied in place to stop it falling off.

This flatbed truck has its own mini **crane** behind the **cab**. The crane lifts cargo on and off the truck. The driver works the crane by moving **levers**.

13

Articulated trucks

An articulated truck bends in the middle to make it easier to go round corners. The part where the **cargo** is carried is called a trailer.

The front part with the driver's **cab** and **engine** is called the tractor unit. It pulls the trailer along. It can be moved from one trailer and attached to another.

Road trains

A road train is an articulated truck with two or three trailers instead of just one. Road trains can often be seen in Australia carrying goods and livestock.

Long-distance trucks like road trains often travel for several days. Inside the **cab** is a bed where the driver sleeps at night. Some trucks also have curtains and cupboards for the driver's clothes.

Tanker trucks

A tanker truck is a truck with a huge **tank** to carry **cargo**. Some tanks can be filled with liquid such as **petrol**. Other tanks carry food such as flour, grain or beans.

The tank is filled up through holes in the top. After the journey, the tank empties out through pipes at the back. The driver opens **valves** to let the cargo out.

Dumper trucks

A monster dumper truck can be as tall as a house. The huge wheels are as tall as the truck driver. Monster dumper trucks do not drive on roads. They work at **quarries** or building sites.

The back of a dumper truck tips up to make its **cargo** slide out on to the ground. Powerful **hydraulic** arms use water pressure to extend and make the back tip.

Rubbish trucks

Many types of truck do a special job instead of carrying **cargo**. This truck goes around the streets collecting rubbish, which it takes to a dump.

A machine lifts rubbish bins and shakes the rubbish from them into the back of the truck. Inside the truck is another machine that crushes the rubbish to make room for more.

Snow ploughs

A snow plough is a special truck that clears ice and snow from roads. During the winter snow ploughs keep roads open so that other vehicles can make their journeys safely.

At the front of the snow plough is a wide metal shovel called a plough. As the snow plough moves along, the plough pushes snow to the side of the road.

Mobile cranes

This truck is called a mobile **crane**. With its sturdy wheels and **tyres**, it can drive on roads or dirt tracks. People can hire mobile cranes when they want heavy objects lifted.

The crane's extending arm is called a boom. It can reach high into the air. The driver operates the crane from a **cab**. Metal feet stop the mobile crane toppling over.

Monster trucks

These amazing vehicles are called
monster trucks. Their owners make them
from ordinary pick-up trucks and race
against each other over bumpy tracks
and obstacle courses.

Monster trucks have huge wheels and strong **suspensions** for landing after jumps. Inside the **cab** are strong bars that protect the driver if the truck rolls over.

Timeline

1769 Frenchman Nicholas Cugnot builds a truck to pull a huge gun. It is the first vehicle powered by a **steam engine**.

1830s Steam-powered coaches are used in England to carry passengers between towns. But they ruin the dirt roads!

1850s Steam-powered traction engines are built to pull farm machinery. Similar trucks are used to pull wagons on the roads.

1885 The first proper car is built in Germany by Karl Benz. It has three wheels and is driven along by a **petrol** engine. Top speed is 13 kilometres per hour.

1892 German engineer Rudolph Diesel develops the diesel engine. Most modern trucks have a diesel engine.

1896 The first proper truck is built in Germany by Gottlieb Daimler. Trucks soon take over from horse-drawn wagons.

1940s The first small four-wheel drive truck, called a Jeep, was built for the US army to use in the Second World War.

Glossary

cab   the space at the front of a truck where the truck driver sits

cargo   goods that are moved from place to place

crane   a machine for lifting large, heavy objects

engine   a machine that powers movement using fuel

fuel   a substance that burns to make heat

hydraulic   moved by a liquid

lever   a rod which tilts up and down or from side to side

petrol   a liquid fuel used in petrol engines

quarry   a place where rock is dug from the ground

rubber   a soft solid material made from chemicals. It is poured into moulds to make tyres.

steam   water that has become a gas

suspension   a system of springs that let a truck's wheels move up and down over bumps

tank   large container for storing something

tyre   a rubber ring that fits around the outside of a wheel. It is filled with air.

valve   a device that opens and closes to let a liquid or a gas flow or stop it flowing

Index

Titles in the *Transport Around The World* series

Hardback 0 431 10840 4

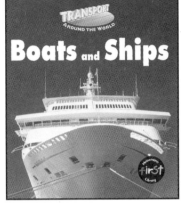

Hardback 0 431 10841 2

Hardback 0 431 10839 0

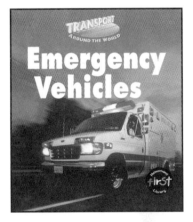

Hardback 0 431 10854 4

Hardback 0 431 10852 8

Hardback 0 431 10838 2

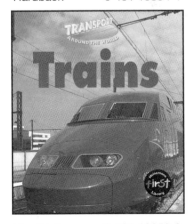

Hardback 0 431 10853 6

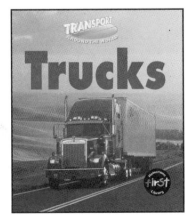

Hardback 0 431 10855 2

Find out about the other titles in this series on our website www.heinemann.co.uk/library